Yoda

Copyright © 2010 by Lucasfilm Ltd. & ® or ™ where indicated.
All Rights Reserved. Used Under Authorization.
Library of Congress Cataloging-in-Publication Data is available.
ISBN: 978-0-8118-7470-0

Manufactured by Starlite Development, Wu Jiang Qu,
Shaoguan, China, in June 2018.
Designed by Michael Morris

20 19 18 17 16 15 14

Chronicle Books LLC
680 Second Street
San Francisco, California 94107
www.chroniclebooks.com

Yoda

Bring you Wisdom, I Will

CHRONICLE BOOKS

SAN FRANCISCO

INTRODUCTION

⚜

Yoda is one of the few known members of a mysterious species. His unassuming size and mischievous personality hide his unparalleled mastery of the Jedi arts. A legendary warrior—albeit the first to tell you that wars do not make one great—and former Grand Master of the Jedi High Council on Coruscant, Yoda is above all a teacher. Nothing gives him greater joy than passing along his wisdom. For over eight hundred years, he taught the Jedi Order's greatest heroes—Mace Windu, Qui-Gon Jinn, and Obi-Wan Kenobi—and one of its most reviled villains, Count Dooku.

Yoda's deep attunement to the Force—a mysterious energy field that binds all living things and gives the Jedi their powers—is due to his advanced age and partly to the hundreds of years he spent exploring the galaxy and studying the Force in its myriad permutations across worlds and cultures. Throughout his travels, Yoda developed a simple yet profound understanding of the Force whose nuances he strives to pass along to his students. He teaches that all are connected and vital to the Force; that one must be mindful of the present, not dwell on the past nor remain fixated on the future; that one stays grounded in reality by accepting what is, not wishing for what may be; that intention without action is meaningless; and that wisdom is within reach of those who are clear-headed and emotionally composed. Probably the most important thing Yoda teaches his students is this: believe in yourself.

In the waning days of the Republic, Yoda recognized threats that lurked both within and without the Jedi Order. A massive Separatist movement was tearing the galaxy asunder, while the reemergence of the Order's ancient enemies, the Dark Lords of the Sith, disrupted the Jedi's connection to the Force. Many Jedi Knights had grown complacent at best, disillusioned and arrogant at worst. This spiritual malaise enabled the Sith to lure the Jedi into a protracted and catastrophic war whose tragic culmination was the eradication of the Order itself as the Jedi were hunted and destroyed by agents of the dark side of the Force.

Yoda was among those persecuted and, with everything he knew, everyone he taught and fought beside gone, he exiled himself to Dagobah, safely hidden from the ruling Sith Lords. And it is there, far away from the jewel of the Republic with its politics, trappings of high culture, and the turmoil of savage war, that Yoda finds solace by communing with the Force. Exploring its mysteries and marveling at its seemingly infinite subtleties, as he waits for a new student—a new hope—who will blaze a path of light through the darkness, ensuring an end to the darkness, and the rebirth of the Jedi Order.

When nine hundred years
old you reach, look as
good you will not.

YODA

Why wish you become Jedi? Hmm?

LUKE

Mostly because of my father,
I guess.

YODA

Ah, your father. Powerful Jedi was he,
powerful Jedi.

What know you of ready?
For eight hundred years
have I trained Jedi.
My own counsel will
I keep on who is
to be trained!

A Jedi must have
the deepest commitment,
the most serious mind.

Clear your mind of questions.

YODA

That place . . . is strong with the
dark side of the Force. A domain of evil
it is. In you must go.

LUKE

What's in there?

YODA

Only what you take with you.

How do you get so big,
eating food of this kind?

Adventure. Heh!
Excitement. Heh!
A Jedi craves not
these things.

Wars not make one great.

Use your feelings, you must.

A Jedi uses the Force for knowledge and defense, never for attack.

LUKE

Is the dark side stronger?

YODA

No . . . no . . . no.
Quicker, easier, more seductive.

Attachment leads to jealousy. The shadow of greed, that is.

Your weapons . . .
you will not need them.

Size matters not. Look at me.
Judge me by my size, do you?

LUKE
I don't believe it.

YODA
That is why you fail.

Control, control. You must learn control.

﹡﹍﹎⚜﹍﹎﹡

Fear is the path to the dark side . . . fear leads to anger . . . anger leads to hate . . . hate leads to suffering.

Train yourself to let go of
everything you fear to lose.

Truly wonderful, the mind of
a child is.

Try not.
Do.
Or do not.
There is no try.

You must feel the Force around you. Here, between you . . . me . . . the tree . . . the rock . . . everywhere!

Hard to see, the dark side is.

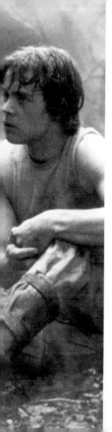

A Jedi's strength flows
from the Force. But
beware of the dark side.
Anger . . . fear . . .
aggression.
The dark side of the
Force are they. Easily
they flow, quick to join
you in a fight.

If once you start down the dark path,
forever will it dominate your destiny;
consume you it will.

LUKE

How am I to know the good side
from the bad?

YODA

You will know. When you are calm,
at peace. Passive.

LUKE

Master, moving stones around is one thing. This is totally different.

YODA

No! No different! Only different in your mind. You must unlearn what you have learned.

Only a fully trained Jedi Knight with the
Force as his ally will conquer Vader and
his Emperor. If you end your training
now, if you choose the quick and easy
path, as Vader did, you will become an
agent of evil.

A little more knowledge might
light our way.

Death is a natural part of life.

Reach out and sense the
Force around you.

The dark side clouds
everything; impossible to
see, the future is.

Through the Force, things you will see.
Other places. The future . . . the past. Old
friends long gone.

The fear of loss is a path to the dark side.

My ally is the Force. And a powerful ally it is. Life creates it; makes it grow. Its energy surrounds us and binds us.

Luminous beings are we . . . not this crude matter.

Always in motion is the future.

Strong is Vader. Mind what you have learned. Save you, it can.

Twilight is upon me, and soon night must fall. That is the way of things . . . the way of the Force.

Rejoice for those around you who transform into the Force.
Mourn them, do not.
Miss them, do not.

No more training do you require.
Already know you that which you need.

Confer on you, the level of Jedi Knight,
the Council does.

Pass on what you have learned.

May the Force be with you.